Living!

Elizabeth Austen

I spy a rock.

not living

I spy a tree.

living

I spy a bench.

not living

I spy a dog.

living

I spy a swing.

not living

I spy a bug.

living

I spy a bike.

not living

I spy me.

Living!

Let's Do Science!

What things are living? Try this!

What to Get

- ❑ paper and pencil
- ❑ pictures of living and not living things

What to Do

1. Group the items into living and not living things.

2. Make a chart like this one. Tape the pictures in the first column. Write an X to show if each thing is living or not living.

3. Tell how living things and not living things are the same and different.

Glossary

living—alive

not living—not alive

Index

Your Turn!

Can you spy three living things in the picture above? Can you spy three not living things?

Consultants

Sally Creel, Ed.D.
Curriculum Consultant

Leann Iacuone, M.A.T., NBCT, ATC
Riverside Unified School District

Jill Tobin
California Teacher of the Year
Semi-Finalist
Burbank Unified School District

Publishing Credits

Conni Medina, M.A.Ed., *Managing Editor*
Lee Aucoin, *Creative Director*
Diana Kenney, M.A.Ed., NBCT, *Senior Editor*
Lynette Tanner, *Editor*
Lexa Hoang, *Designer*
Hillary Dunlap, *Photo Editor*
Rachelle Cracchiolo, M.S.Ed., *Publisher*

Image Credits: p.6 ARvind Balaraman/age Fotostock; p.24 Lexa Hoang; pp.10, 22 iStock; pp.18–19 (illustrations) Rusty Kinnunen; all other images from Shutterstock.

Library of Congress Cataloging-in-Publication Data

Austen, Elizabeth (Elizabeth Charlotte), author.
Living! / Elizabeth Austen.
pages cm
Summary: "It is time to learn about living things."—
Provided by publisher.
Audience: K to grade 3.
Includes index.
ISBN 978-1-4807-4520-9 (pbk.) —
ISBN 978-1-4807-5129-3 (ebook)
1. Life (Biology)—Juvenile literature.
2. Readers (Primary) I. Title.
QH309.2.A97 2015
570—dc23

2014008605

Teacher Created Materials
5301 Oceanus Drive
Huntington Beach, CA 92649-1030
http://www.tcmpub.com

ISBN 978-1-4807-4520-9